Mone

How to Turn Your Smartphone into a Six Figure Money-Making Marketing Machine and Close BIG Deals Quickly and Easily with Mobile Text and Video Marketing

Version 4.1
By Mike Koenigs
11-Time #1 Bestselling Author

FREE - Bonus Training

This book includes **step-by-step video training** and **copy-paste scripts** you can use RIGHT NOW to find **prospects and close 4, 5 and 6-figure deals**!

No software, experience or list required!
Get it NOW at www.GoMoneyPhone.com

Table of Contents

Introduction: Welcome to Money Phone!	5
Endorsements and Accolades	9
Overview and Explanation of This Book	12
The Secret Sauce: Micro-Commitments	18
The Process Explained	24
Here's the Formula Structure That Leads to a Close	36
BONUS! Super-Simple, Free Leads!	40
The Six Figure Text Message Method	43
Networking Without a Business Card Template	45
More Example Video Proposals	51
Example Script: Consult and Profit	52
Free Masterclass - How to Get 3-5 High Ticket Consulting Deals Each Month With Reliability & Predictability… Even If You've NEVER Had A Consulting Client Before!	54
Example Script: Publish and Profit Live Event	56
Example Script: Celebrity Bootcamp	60
Step 1: Context, Framing and "I heard you and know what's wrong"	61
Step 2: The Pitch (this can be pre-recorded)	61
Become a Celebrity in Only 48 Hours!	63

©2017 Mike Koenigs and You Everywhere Now
Get the Free Money Phone Bonus Video at www.GoMoneyPhone.com

Example Script: Speak and Profit	66
Step 1: Context, Framing and "I heard you and know what's wrong"	70
Step 2: The Pitch	70
Learn the Most Valuable Skill that Produces Bigger, Faster Deals & Income Per Hour than Anything	72
Example Script: Create and Profit	73
Step 1: Context, Framing and "I heard you and know what's wrong"	74
Step 2: The Pitch (this can be pre-recorded)	75
How to Make Profitable Products in Only 48 Hours	77
Summary, Implementation and Action Steps	79
Make $$$ with Webcasts, Webinars & Facebook Live!	82
Where's the Money This Year? Join us for a Business, Marketing, Opportunities & Tech Predictions Show to Grow Your Business!	85
It's Time for You to Go Live and Profit!	87
About Mike Koenigs	91
Book Mike Koenigs to Speak	93

FREE Bonus Masterclass

If you **want to Get 3-5 High Ticket Consulting Deals Each Month with Reliability & Predictability**...*Even If You've NEVER Had A Consulting Client Before,* **join me for a free masterclass:** www.yen.tv/CAPWebinar

Introduction: Welcome to Money Phone!

Thank you! This book represents nearly 20 years of hard work, experience and effort of my incredible team and customers. Maybe you're one of them!

My goal for you is simple: to help you earn more money in less time while increasing the size and quantity of the transactions. As long as you're motivated, implementation-minded and able to model the system I present for your business, you'll understand the concepts 15-20 minutes from now and can start generating interest and deals in an hour or two.

If you have a short attention span, have ADD (like me) or learn better and faster with video, make sure to head over to **www.GoMoneyPhone.com** because you can watch a video that explains and demonstrates everything in this book in about 45 minutes.

If you DON'T have a list or customer database, jump ahead to the chapter, "**BONUS! Super-Simple, Free Leads!**" because that will show you where you can access 20-100 highly qualified leads right now.

Here is what to expect in this book so you get the most out of it and your expectations are met.

First, it's interactive. There are lots of opportunities for you to go deeper into the content, gain access to free training videos, participate in some free interactive masterclass events and more.

Second, this book is for business. It's intended to help you grow your business, produce qualified leads and make money. Quickly.

Third, it's for implementers. There are LOTS of ideas that you can use right now to grow any business, in any industry, country or language, anywhere in the world. If you're the type who's looking for free, easy money, this isn't the book for you. I'm not here to blow smoke up your butt and lie to you.

Fourth, this book wasn't intended to be a NY Times #1 Bestseller. It's designed to start a conversation with you, give you and me a chance to get to know each other better, develop trust, a bond and ultimately help us decide if we will work together someday.

Fifth, this is a book that's short, but packed with implementable content and lots of ideas. My intention and the purpose of this book is to show you the most powerful ways to market yourself, generate qualified leads, close deals and leverage the latest technology and strategies available and set yourself up for long-term growth and maybe sell your business in the future. We have a how-to system available that includes everything you need to execute what you read in these pages.

I'll be the first to admit, I'm a shameless self-promoter - and I want to help you reach more people, make more money and add value to your life and everyone you encounter. You'll notice there are opportunities throughout this book to watch free training videos and YES, I do have some great products you can invest in to amplify your message and make more money. They work and I've helped over 50,000 people in 121 countries with my products and services so I'm certain they'll help you too.

Having said that, if you like what you read, *or most of what you read*, I'd absolutely, positively love to hear from you, get to know you better and have you post a success story, picture or video and comment on my Facebook wall at **www.Facebook.com/MikeAKoenigs**.

The BEST way to start a relationship with me will be to visit the web links in this book, join me for the free training masterclasses, and learn more about how to grow your business and brand. It's my pleasure to help you make money, change lives and gain more freedom!

Sincerely,
Mike Koenigs, La Jolla, California, USA

PS - I wrote and edited this book myself. There are probably some spelling, grammatical and layout errors. If you find one, will you do me a favor and tell me what you find by sending me an email to **MikeKoenigs@gmail.com**? Just note the page number, sentence and mistake and I'll fix it right away *and thank you for your help*. I'm all about results, implementation and speed and chose to give you tools that make you money over perfection and procrastination. **Money loves speed and time kills deals!**

PPS - if you love this book or make money because of it, will you please post a review on Amazon at **www.YEN.tv/MoneyPhoneReview**? If you DON'T like it, send me an email, tell me why and I'll give you your money back, ok?

Please be kind. I have a son. He reads what people say about me online and so do his friends. There's no sense in dragging an innocent kid into something unnecessary. Nobody likes a bully and our world has too much hate in it the way it is. Let's be friends. Cool?

PPPS - If you enjoy this book, find it useful, I'll be very grateful if you post a short review and your success story on Amazon. Your support makes a difference and I read and respond to all the reviews personally so I can make this book even better. If you'd like to leave a review, just visit this link: **www.YEN.tv/MoneyPhoneReview**.

Thanks again! **Let's close some deals!**

Endorsements and Accolades

"Mike is an extraordinary man. He's brought me insights on how to reach people on the Internet that are incredibly valuable. This is a man you should deal with. Take advantage of what he has to offer."
Tony Robbins, World Authority on Leadership Psychology and the nation's #1 Life and Business Strategist

"There are those who lead and those who follow and then there are trend creators. Mike is a true leader who uses his creative genius and relentless pursuit of new frontiers and technologies to change the landscape of what is possible and usable in today's crazy, ever-changing business landscape."
John Assaraf, NY Times Bestselling Author, CEO NeuroGym.com

"Mike Koenigs is the "Doc" Brown of marketing automation and technology. One question or problem unlocks his brain and 20 to 30 ingenious ideas pour out of it. Some are OMG! Others are WTF? But there is  always one or two that are worth a fortune. One idea grew my database from 30,000 to 800,000 in 14 months. Another one contributed to a product launch that generated a million dollars in three days. Most recently another contributed to a marketing automation process that is now generating $250,00 a week. So yes, like "Doc" Brown, if you can get past the crazy outfits and wild hair, Mike Koenigs is a brilliant marketing muse that can make you money!"
Darren Hardy, Founding Publisher/Editor SUCCESS magazine and Mentor to CEOs and High-Performance Achievers

"I feel very blessed to have Mike Koenigs as a friend and in my personal and business life. After many years of teaching people around the world, it is guys like Mike Koenigs that keeps me sharp. And, we both share the same  goals of wanting to help millions of entrepreneurs achieve their goals to greater financial and business success. More people need to engage in Mike's teachings – quite amazing!"
Brian Tracy, Author, Speaker, Entrepreneur

"There are very few visionaries who can truly predict the future and pluck from thin air the next big thing, not just once, but time after time - Tom Peters, Faith Popcorn, Sean Parker. Mike

Koenigs breathes that rarified air. Mike not only sees the future, he monetizes it. I've seen Mike take his vision and turn it into a successful million dollars plus business in less than 100 days eleven times! Whether he is teaching based on actual results (not theory), simplifying complex systems into digestible bites, extracting the genius from interviews with the most interesting people in the world or selling millions in front of the camera, I can think of no one better equipped to share with you the actionable knowledge Mike has distilled into his latest book."
Roland Frasier - CEO, All Channels Media

"Mike Koenigs and I are in a mastermind group together and I have known him for several years. He is without question one of the smartest marketers I know. He's also one of the most deliberate, studied, systematic, focused and scientific entrepreneurs I know. I would recommend anything Mike produces because it is always top quality and delivers massive value. When it comes to business, he's the guy you want to be when you grow up :)"
Glen Ledwell CEO & Co Founder, Mind Movies LLC

"Mike never ceases to amaze me with his ability to spot and capitalize cutting-edge business and marketing trends and then turn around and make it simple for anyone else to do the same. From the tools he creates to the training he provides, Mike knows what it takes to succeed quickly. I have often found myself asking "What would Mike Do?" Instead of reinventing the wheel, I simply steer it in his direction. Many people achieve success, only a few people can lead others to success as well as Mike Koenigs."
Brad Costanzo, CEO of Costanzo Marketing Group

Overview and Explanation of This Book

What is Money Phone and how will it change the way you do business?

Every business needs to get and close deals as quickly as possible but usually have these challenges (how many of these sounds like you?):

They (or you) don't:

- ✓ Have a prospect or customer list
- ✓ Know where to find high-quality, qualified prospects
- ✓ Have time
- ✓ Have resources and budgets
- ✓ Know how to pitch their products and services the right way
- ✓ Have good marketing
- ✓ Have an advertising budget
- ✓ Have a tech team
- ✓ Have automated marketing tools

Money Phone is the solution for all of these challenges because with it and your smartphone, you can:

- Start closing deals an hour from now
- Get qualified leads **IMMEDIATELY for FREE**
- Find high-quality, motivated prospects with money
- Use step-by-step scripts adaptable for any business
- Work without a marketing or advertising budget
- Do this yourself, no employees required

- Start with just your smartphone and automate later
- Use Money Phone to close deals of any size - $500, $1,000, $10,000, $100,000 or even more

Money phone uses a combination of simple text messages, short 1 minute videos and advanced psychology (but not icky, annoying, salesy tactics) to access high-quality prospects, get their attention, engage with them, gain their trust and get them to say YES faster than any other marketing system in the world.

If you can copy and paste, send a text message, take a picture and shoot a 1 minute video on your smartphone while you read a short script, Money Phone can make you money starting now.

If you're impatient or learn faster by watching and doing and want me to show you step-by-step how to DO everything in this book with real-life scripts, head over to **www.GoMoneyPhone.com** right now for the free 45 minute interactive training video.

In the video, you'll see the EXACT strategies and get the EXACT scripts I've used to close $2,700, $7,700, $19,000 and $81,000 deals with text messages, short videos and a smartphone. If you don't have a list, you'll love this bonus because you can start getting and closing deals right away.

Who am I and why should you listen to or trust me?

I've been consulting, advising, building, growing and selling businesses since I was 16 years old. I've helped over 50,000 businesses over the course of 30 years who have purchased my products, coaching and consulting services and software tools. Over the course of my career, I've sold over $50,000,000 worth of products, services, coaching, consulting and advice. I sold two of my businesses to publicly-traded companies.

I think it's reasonable to say I've witnessed and participated in a multitude of different ways to find, get and close lots of customers. What excites me the most is combining mobile marketing with video to close deals in minutes instead of days or weeks and that's what this book and companion video is all about.

With this strategy AND the "Mobile Money Marketing" bonus that's included with the **Consult and Profit** program (**visit www.YEN.tv/CAPWebinar for details**), you can close 4, 5 and even SIX FIGURE deals in minutes!

When you use this strategy, and automate it with a mobile text marketing system like **Skipio**, you can make even more! *BTW - you can get a free trial of the* **Skipio** *mobile text marketing system for free* when you text the word **Tryit** to (858) 375-1444 or go to **www.TrySkipio.com.**

Make sure you check out the "BONUS! Super-Simple, Free Leads!" chapter in this book for free lead sources (**www.GoMoneyPhone.com** will take you there).

Everything in this book and video works face-to-face in person, at live events, conferences, trade shows, associations, in retail or online. The principles are all the same.

So why go to **REAL PLACES**? Because **THAT'S WHERE THE MONEY IS**. Trade shows, conferences, live events and associations are filled with people who traveled, paid for a hotel, an event ticket, have taken time away from their business and families and expect an outcome or result, they want to get exposed to new tools, resources, people or ideas. The promoter paid a small (or huge) fortune to get those people in a room - and for every 100 people at an event, most likely 10,000 or more received marketing materials to entice them attend. The audience is the "Crème de la Crème" in terms of prospect value and with the right finesse, you can ethically hijack them straight into your business.

You can bypass years of business and list-building, prospecting and creating an infrastructure into a couple of hours and walk away with tens or hundreds of thousands of dollars in business with zero risk.

These strategies **WILL work online and with Facebook ads or any other media marketing** - but I want to say up front and on the record, that *only fools believe they can sit behind their laptop computers in their underwear making "free money."* In my experience, you need to get your message in front of 100 to 1,000 people on Facebook for every lead you get that might convert into a sale compared to 1 in 5 at an event.

Let me break this down for you in real-world numbers...

Forgive me if the next couple of paragraphs lose you if you're not a marketing geek...

If you advertise on Facebook, you'll pay between $0.50-$2.00 for a click from a qualified prospect. If you have an automated marketing system in place, this will translate into spending $500 to $1,000 on a $2,000 sale. Speaking from experience, it takes 30-90 days of preparation to build an automated marketing funnel that can cost $5,000-$50,000 or more to create, build and test. In contrast, I can go to an event that's PACKED with highly qualified prospects for less than $1,000 and close $10,000 to $50,000 (or more) in deals in one day with the strategies and scripts in this book.

To be clear, I'm assuming you and I are selling coaching, consulting, advising, products or services that cost $1,000-$25,000 or more. If you're selling cheap products or services, I highly recommend you STOP whatever you're doing and get into the business of selling big-ticket items.

Money Loves Speed. Time Kills Deals. What would you rather do - get a deal TODAY or risk 90 days and potentially $50,000 creating a sales funnel that might not work?

Using mobile text marketing to generate big-ticket sales requires several simple strategies that I'll share and discuss with a variety of demonstrations that are all based on real-life scenarios. In other words, I've used the exact words and scripts in this book to close hundreds of thousands of dollars worth of deals.

The scripts practically guarantee you'll get engagement, responses and action nearly 100% of the time. Let's close some deals right now!

The Secret Sauce: Micro-Commitments

Big Idea #1: "Micro-commitments." These are simple, short text messages that engage a prospect or someone you know in an authentic conversation that is natural and doesn't come across as being contrived, salesy, slimy or needy.

What are micro-commitments? They're simple one-sentence messages that encourage a non-committal response that results in a longer conversation and ends with genuine engagement and *ideally a sale*.

More importantly, you'll know in minutes or seconds when your prospect is reacting and responding to you in REAL-TIME. Unlike email, which gets opened 5%-20% of the time if you're lucky and 5%-20% of the time gets clicked through (these are real industry standards BTW). **In comparison according to numerous studies, 96% of mobile text messages get read within 10 minutes after being sent.**

In the world of marketing, **you have 2 seconds to grab someone's attention**. If your audience is interested in what they see or hear, you might get **20 seconds of their time**. If that's good, you can probably get **2 minutes**.

And if you earn 20-50 minutes of someone's time, you can probably **influence and persuade almost anyone to begin a relationship and buy something from you**.

In the Money Phone strategy, you don't need 20, 10 or 5 minutes to get and close a deal. These scripts can make deals happen in as little as 1-2 minutes!

Here are four examples of micro-commitment messages that are personal and encourage an immediate response with minutes to ethically persuade or influence someone to buy from you:

- "Hi Bill! Checking in - do you need anything from me today?"
- "Hey Bill, great meeting you today. Here's that picture of us. I'll follow up after the event ends."
- "Hi Bill, are you still interested in _____?"
- "Hey Bill, I was looking through my phone and found this picture of us from the ____ conference. I was just thinking about you. How are things?" (include a photo from your camera roll)

These messages aren't salesy and encourage an immediate response. The reason this is so important is because we are all busy and as a marketer, **getting someone's attention is the #1 hardest thing to do**.

If you can get someone's attention and engage with them conversationally, they are much more likely to be open to your offer without you coming across as being salesy.

When your prospect is engaged, reading your message and responding, you're 90% past the hump. On any smartphone, you can tell when someone is reading and responding to a text because there's a little indicator that shows they are replying — here it is:

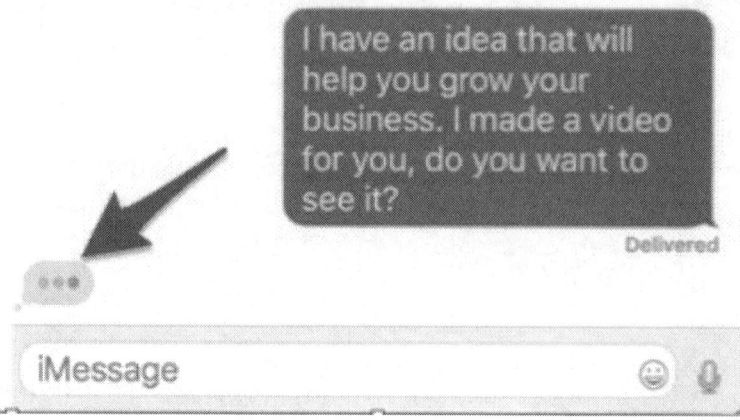

THIS is the most important and valuable piece of information you as a marketer or salesperson can ever get: **THEY'RE ENGAGED RIGHT NOW**. You've hooked them, they're curious, they're paying attention - and THAT is what a micro-commitment is all about.

Think about it: if you sent a micro-commitment message to 20 people and you see 15 "response indicators", that's more than likely more immediate activity that you can get from mailing a massive list...

There is a super-easy way to go from "attention-engage-close". It doesn't require special equipment other than the smartphone in your pocket, can be automated with software tools (I'll give you a free trial to the system I use) and you can teach anyone in your organization how to do the busy-work for you if you don't want to do it yourself.

This strategy also works with Facebook Messenger, Twitter, Skype, WhatsApp, SnapChat or any other direct message application your prospect is using. The key factor is you need them to be interacting with you in real-time for this process to work effectively.

If you've watched me speak, you've seen me teach a **simple one-sentence "hook" that will grab almost anyone's attention** and is also a perfect way to sign a book or business card.

The simple sentence is:

"I have an idea that will help you _____."

Depending on the business, service or product you provide, the last part of the sentence can be:

- Grow your business
- Close a deal in 5 minutes
- Lose 20 pounds
- Capture more leads
- Market with social media
- Save $20,000 or more on your tax bill this year
- Raise money for your foundation
- Get 20%-50% more people to show up at your next live event
- Close 2x-3x more deals a week
- Become a bestselling author in just 3 days
- Get paid while you make an information product

Or any benefit that you or your company promise.

Just to make sure I don't forget anything and follow up with the prospect with integrity and accuracy, I make a point of taking notes or recording the conversation (with permission of course) when I meet a new person I can help grow their business, get more leads, become a best-selling author, help them multiply their income, value, authority or start a new business.

I listen, ask lots of questions and pay close attention to any point of pain and challenges they have in their business while asking myself this question: "How can I help this person? Who or what do I know that could solve this person's challenge *right now*?"

Whenever possible, I capture all of their contact information with my <u>Networking Without a Business Card Form</u> and <u>"Call Me" Survey</u>. This gives me all the information I need to know what people want and what their business challenges and pains are.

Bonus Follow Up Tools

Visit **www.YEN.tv/CallMe** to get my "Networking Without a Business Card" form or see how I automate the process by texting **"Call Me"** to **(858) 213-0030**.

I make certain to get the person's name, title, email, mobile #, web address and company name at a minimum.

There's a great saying that a mentor of mine once said:

"He or she who diagnoses the disease is the first to be able to prescribe a cure."

When you *win the role of being "doctor"* to anyone, you earn the right to *diagnose and cure*.

When you ask great questions, people assume you have the answers. As an advisor or doctor, you're instantly placed in a position of authority, power and trust.

The Process Explained

Next, I'll guide you through multiple variations of this system beginning with an "in person" process that's loaded with powerful psychology. As we go through the scripts, it's going to get easier and you'll notice the scripts will allow you to get and close deals without even speaking directly to a prospect in many cases!

What I want to *impress upon you* is the importance of **understanding your MARKET and getting to understand the LANGUAGE that market uses** so you can connect with the right **MESSAGE** and convert this opportunity into a sale. You might need to watch my video training (at www.GoMoneyPhone.com) or read this section a couple of times to comprehend the psychology. Once you've absorbed it, you'll be able to quickly implement this process in your own business in as little as a day to get and close big deals.

When I meet someone in person at an event and determine that they have a business, have a problem that I can solve with one of my products, services, connections, introductions, referrals, relationships or advice, I start asking them diagnostic questions. Make sure you invest your time on qualified prospects! These are the people who have trade show booths, are in breakout sessions, attending speaking sessions or workshops.

If they've spent money and want a specific outcome, they're a qualified prospect.

Here are some example questions you can ask that are sales and marketing related:

- Who are you? What do you do? What does [company name] do?
- OR, if they are at a trade show booth: What is your product? How does it work? What does it do?
- Who is your product for? Who is your ideal customer?
- Can you tell me a story about how [ideal customer] has used your product successfully?
- How or where do you find your best customers *right now*?
- *Who specifically* are some people or companies you're working with (I ask for specific names)
- What's working best for you to get and close customers?
- How do you know when what you're doing to get customers is working?
- How much does it cost to get a new customer?
- What is the biggest challenge you are experiencing right now in your sales process?
- What have you done to fix that challenge?
- What other challenges are you experiencing in your business?
- What else? What else?

The reason I ask "what else" multiple times is to get a list of every possible challenge or problem they might be having. I ask that question over and over again until they say "I can't think of anything else" or I can tell I'm starting to lose rapport. By getting a list of challenges, I'll gain a substantial number of potential "hooks" or ways to help them - and possibilities and reasons to follow up with them later.

Note: no matter what business or profession you're in, the process of getting and closing deals is the same. Your specific questions might be different, but use your imagination or study some diagnostic or industry specific sales guides for your niche to come up with great questions. I can't stress this enough - and it's the SINGLE BIGGEST challenge people have when adapting this strategy to their business:

THIS PROCESS WILL WORK FOR YOU AND IN YOUR BUSINESS!
This process works *when you implement it*!

After using this diagnostic strategy for years, I can zero in on practically any business or personal challenge and get a high-level person engaged and to answer everything I need to know in five minutes or less to sell them something and be in a high state of rapport with them. It takes practice, but the real secret to selling anything is to *ask great questions, shut up and listen*.

When you do this, people feel as though you have the answers and can solve their problems. I can't stress this enough - asking GREAT questions gives you enormous power.

I'm a numbers guy - so I ask "money" questions like "how much does it cost you to get a new customer or close a deal?" If that person is selling a $10,000 product and they tell me it costs them $2,500 to get a customer or close a deal, I know for a fact that they'll pay that amount of money all day long for new customers - maybe more. I know at that moment that I could easily propose a $10,000 fee if I could reasonably assure or show them how to get 4 sales which would pay for my fees. (My consulting rates are $5,000 per hour and $30,000 per day)

This is how you qualify your prospects. After asking a couple questions and getting a few responses, you're going to know if there's an opportunity worth pursuing in a couple minutes. Depending on the industry you're in, you simply do some simple math in your head:

- How big is the problem? (Pain)
- How much does it currently cost to solve that problem? (Money)
- How many opportunities are there to solve that problem per day/week or month? (Frequency / quantity)

If you can solve more of those problems for less money, faster or more effectively than they are right now, there's an opportunity for both of you and the conversation is worth continuing!

The single MOST IMPORTANT challenge has already been answered - and that is whether or not this is a *qualified prospect or candidate*. They're at the event - so they're spending money to eliminate their challenges. If they're a decision-maker, they're qualified.

In my specific case, I have self-study digital training products that start at $1,997 that help people solve business challenges and provide business coaching, consulting and advising services that start at $20,000 and go as high as $100,000 and sometimes more. I've included my product catalog and many of my sales scripts as examples in this book that you can model for your business.

When I identify a "right fit" client, I simply say, "I have some ideas that will solve x, y and z problems for you." If I can close them on the spot, great, but I wait a couple days to close on a $20,000 or larger deal.

I just need some basic information to follow up - and provide a way to convert this new prospect into a buyer quickly and easily.

Here's one way I do this:

I take a picture of their business card with my phone, take a selfie picture with them or I shoot a short video of us smiling, having fun or engaging in some way. I want people to remember having an emotional, happy and connected experience with me. While building rapport, I ask them some personal questions - where do they live, how many kids do they have, how did they meet their spouse, where are they from, what college did they attend, etc. At some point, we're going to make some kind of connection or find a thing we have in common that creates a connection or bond.

Michael Gerber, Author of the E-Myth

If I shoot a short video, I'll say something memorable about our conversation, "Hi Bill, this is Mike Koenigs. We're both from Minnesota. We're here at the *Event Name* and have been talking about *Common Interest*. You told me about challenge, objection, challenge, objection and I have an idea about how to fix that with *My Solution*. I'll think about this a bit more and follow up with you after the event."

After taking the picture or video, I send that picture or video right away along with my contact information and let them know I will follow up a day or two after the event ends.

I continue repeating the networking process until I have 10 or 20 connections. Then I walk to an area that has memorable event branding and record a short video for each person that I will send to them right away or *after* the event ends, when they are at home or in their office, away from all the noise and overwhelm.

I make that sending decision based on the level of commitment, interest or conversation I had with that person. If they're super hot to get going, I'll send it right away.

The pictures and videos don't need to be perfect, just memorable!

That video goes something like this:

> "Hi Bill, it was great meeting you at the Event Name on Friday in Las Vegas. I've been thinking about you and your business and I have a couple ideas about how I can help you get more clients and close them faster and for less money. In fact, I'm

absolutely positive I can help you close more live event sales leads with a system I designed that is being used by Darren Hardy from Success Magazine and XPrize Founder, Peter Diamandis. You told me you know you're leaving between $15,000-$35,000 or more on the table at every event and you don't have a system that works consistently. I will follow up with you on Monday with an idea that I think you'll like. Safe travels home."

Notice I included where we met, when we met, something valuable I could provide him and something specific he shared with me about him and his business. The language pattern that's especially important is "you told me..." - this associates Bill with his identity and his integrity when you follow up with him.

To Bill, this is an indication that I pay close attention to what he says and listened to him carefully about what his biggest challenge is. I also make a promise that I am going to follow up and there's nothing HE needs to do!

This creates a friction-free, commitment-free relationship. I'm making it easy for him to say "yes" in every conversation we have in the future. And, more importantly, he won't deny he said that because his ego and identity is attached to this conversation.

Again, I feel this is important to mention because the most common objection I get to this is "well, I'm not a marketing person...my business is different, blah, blah, blah." That's complete and utter nonsense - **every**

business interaction and deal is the same: Get attention, gain rapport, trust, authority status, diagnose challenge, present offer.

Now - this is optional, but very powerful. You want to provide social proof that your product or service works and is being used by someone they know or respect. By doing this, you're going to overcome buying objections right away. Once you've implemented or have done something that's being used successfully by other people (especially influencers in a niche or category), drop those names because it gives you expert and authority status.

My example was "*In fact, I'm absolutely positive I can help you close more live event sales leads with a system I designed that is being used by Darren Hardy and Peter Diamandis.*"(if you don't know who Darren Hardy or Peter Diamandis is, look them up in Google, they're both big influencers in their respective niches).

The next step is THE key to the process. This happens a couple days later - generally two days after an event ends so they have time to recover from the trip but not so long that they don't remember you or the urgency of your conversation and how excited they were when you first spoke. You want to re-associate <u>you</u> with the possible <u>outcome or result</u> that you talked about when you first met.

You don't want to begin a conversation with an offer or any kind of commitment. You just want to know if they are available and paying attention to their phone. If you do the next part incorrectly, you could blow the opportunity or at least slow down the process considerably.

On the day I promise to follow up, I send a really short and noncommittal message:

"Hi Bill, it was great meeting you at the Event Name. Here's that other picture I took of us. We're a couple of good-looking guys, don't you think? ;)"

The last part of the message is a bit humorous – obviously I only say something like that if I know we're in rapport and I feel I have permission to make a light-hearted joke.

I will attach the selfie picture of him and me to that message. It's super personal, friendly and invokes a reaction or response.

Now you wait. At this point he will most likely respond with a short message that goes something like this: "great meeting you too, thanks for the picture."

Now you want to send a really short video that is 30 seconds to one minute long in length. Here is an example scripted message I follow up with to initiate a phone conversation.

> "Hey Bill, I'm glad we reconnected. I've been thinking more about our conversation at the Event Name and I'm absolutely certain I have a solution for that challenge you have closing trade show leads with a lot less effort. I know you were looking

for a way to capture that lost money and I know exactly what you need to make that happen. I can tell you what it is in a short conversation. I just got off the phone and have 5 minutes before my next call. Will right now work for you?"
OR
"Just let me know and I'll send you a short one-minute video that describes you need to know."

Now wait for a response - if you requested a call, they'll reply "OK" OR they'll say something like "sure, send me the video..."

That's your invitation to follow up with the "close."

If you're confused, keep reading. It's normal. I'll make this even easier as we move through the process.

Get More Clients NOW

If YOU want to get attention, stand out and become a trusted person of influence, you NEED this masterclass RIGHT NOW to gain an unfair advantage and competitive edge to promote and market your business, reach celebrity status, attract better customers, make more money and help a lot of people.

Visit **www.YEN.tv/PAPWebinar** to watch the free training event right now.

Here's the Formula Structure That Leads to a Close

Now that you've initiated the connection, conversation and provided context and framing for who you are, what you do, what you can do for them, you just need to make a simple offer.

You've been doing something we call "seeding" the whole time - clearly indicating you or your product is the solution and immediate pain relief for a problem he or she shared with you the first time you connected.

Here's the basic close formula:

Hi [name] - [build rapport], I have THREE things for you:

1. **MIND READING**: Tell them what they want, restate what you discussed when you met (busy people have budgets)
2. **MAIN COURSE**: How we can work together to [get result x]
3. **CALL TO ACTION**: What to do next (I'll do everything for you)

You need to assume they might show the video to someone else if they're not the sole decision-maker, so you need to provide and repeat all the details you've shared in other communications so this message is COMPLETE.

Assume NOTHING. Assume they don't remember ONE THING you've shared with him. Don't even assume they remember meeting you or talking to you or anything you've discussed in your previous messages. If this person is too busy to remember anything, that's a GOOD THING. Don't take anything personally.

Busy Business People have BUDGETS!

HAVING SAID ALL THAT, HERE'S A VIDEO PROPOSAL THAT CAN LEAD TO A CLOSE:

"Hi Bill, when we had our first conversation at the Event Name, you mentioned the challenges you have closing prospects and leads at trade shows. I have a solution that will work for you. The system is being used by Darren Hardy from Success Magazine who grew his list from 30,000 to 800,000. XPrize founder Peter Diamandis captured over 8,000 leads in one day that grew to over 100,000 people in six months. I'm positive this will work for you too. Based on the numbers you shared with me of capturing an average of 150 leads a day but only connecting with 20 after your events are over, I believe you'll be able to double or triple your sales in the next 30 days with the system. It'll take less than 5 minutes to fill you in on the details to get you started. I just got off the phone and have 5 minutes before my next call. Will right now work for you?"
OR
> "Just let me know and I'll send you a one-minute video that describes everything you need to know."

That's the structure of a full 1-minute video proposal:

- Where we met / context and framing
  (I'm not a stranger, I'm safe)
- Restate problems they are having
  (I understand you)
- If you have it, include social proof your system works (It will work for you, it worked for other people, this is a safe decision. If you've worked with someone they know, respect, influences them, they admire or a celebrity uses this product or service, mention that)
- Mention specific results they can experience when they use your product or service-so they can experience "results in advance"
  ("this is what it will feel like when it works for you")
- Low commitment to move forward
  (I'll send you a video, I'll do all the work)
- What to do next
  (give me a call, write me back, request the video)

When they reply, you pick up the phone and close them on the spot, send the close video OR send a link to buy right now. This works like a charm!

Important: If you're thinking that some of what I put in this last message is repetitive, it's because I want every video to stand-alone and not require that my prospect look backwards in time to remember any details or have an excuse to delay deciding or making a buying decision. I also want to make it easy for the prospect to share or show **one video** to another decision-maker without requiring an explanation or pre-frame for that person about what this sales conversation is all about.

In other words, don't assume anyone can tell your story clearly. They can't. They won't. Even an advocate will ruin your sales opportunity unintentionally.

Your goal is to get a buyer to make a decision NOW. If you include everything they need in one place, you'll close the deal faster.

Remember: **Money Loves Speed. Time Kills Deals.**

BONUS! Super-Simple, Free Leads!

Right now, you have 20-100 leads and many of them will convert directly into customers in 12-48 hours if you are willing to suspend your disbelief of what I'm about to share with you for a moment.

These leads are already in your possession; they are pre-qualified and are waiting for you to get their attention, build rapport and put an offer in front of them. Where are these leads you ask? In your phone, right now.

Unless you're a complete wallflower and never leave your house or haven't spoken with anyone in the past three years, over the past 3-36 months, I can positively guarantee you've met someone, exchanged contact information and a text message, had every intention of following up with that person but never did.

With a tiny bit of attention getting and rapport building, you can easily "tickle" them back into being hungry and qualified when you follow these simple directions. Get ready for your "Money Phone" to make you money!

1. Get a pen and a notebook
2. Put your phone in AIRPLANE MODE so you don't get interrupted
3. Set a countdown timer or alarm for 20 minutes on your phone or computer
4. Click through your text messages and scroll backwards through people you've messaged over the past 12-36 months
5. Look for people you've met, connected with, had every intention of following up with but didn't.
6. Write down that person's name along with a rating of 1-10 on their value as a prospect - 10 if they have a problem you can solve, they have money or a budget and you feel you'll be in rapport quickly and easily.
7. Continue until your timer ends
8. If you're on a roll and you have more names to go and your messages and leads are strong, KEEP GOING! You might find that there are hundreds of potential hot leads in your phone!
9. **REPEAT. DO NOT GET DISTRACTED OR TEXT ANYONE UNTIL YOU ARE FINISHED!**
10. Review the list - and prepare to start engaging the high-value people first using the "Micro-commitment" strategy and the "Six Figure Text Message Shortcut Message Method"

That's it! You should be able to engage a significant percentage of these leads and close them in 24-48 hours! Use the scripts, templates, proposals in **Consult and Profit** to get those deals!

Next Step: Close More Deals
Free Masterclass Training

How To Get 3-5 High Ticket Consulting Deals Each Month With Reliability & Predictability... Even If You've NEVER Had A Consulting Client Before!

Visit **www.YEN.tv/CAPWebinar** watch the free training event right now.

The Six Figure Text Message Method

Now that you've gone through your phone and have a list of qualified leads, here is a message sequence to send to them to generate interest and open a sales conversation in 3 quick messages:

1. "Checking in - do you need anything from me today?"
2. "Quick question. Are you still interested in [result]?"
3. "I have an idea that will help you _____ (grow your business, etc.). I made a short video for you, do you want to see it?"

The first message is the "micro-commitment" message. It initiates a conversation, even if you haven't connected with that person in weeks, months or years.

If they don't remember who you are, you can just send them a short little blurb "I'm the guy/gal who helps _____ get/do _____ even if they."

Example: "I'm the guy who will help you get attention, grow your audience, close more deals and charge more for your products and services even if you hate to sell."

Then send message #2 - you're almost certain to get a response. Nobody likes to leave a conversation unfinished - this is called the "Zeigarnik Effect" (Google it). The bottom line is an unfinished conversation creates tension the human brain wants to resolve. Your prospect will feel compelled to answer you.

And when you send message #3, you can initiate the close process.

From this point - it's a numbers game. Every business is a math problem. You present an offer to a certain number of people. If 2 out of 10 buy from you, you know your close ratio is 20%.

And once you "know your numbers", you can automate your marketing and start buying traffic and media to scale your business.

Keep reading - the next chapter shows you how I capture more leads at events. The next chapters are sample 1 minute closing scripts I use in my business when I meet qualified prospects.

Before we go there, I want to explain why I don't carry business cards and why you shouldn't either.

Networking Without a Business Card Template

How do I get people to play by my rules and call me instead of ME chasing them down? *By networking without a business card.* This is a simple process that works like crazy. Recently I closed $87,650 worth of business in two days at a live event.

BUSINESS CARDS SUCK! Not all business cards, but let's face it, most of the time when someone asks for a business card or you exchange one NOTHING HAPPENS! Neither of you follows up because neither of you knows what the other person really needs!

What if there was a way to stand out, get attention and turn every "exchange" into a follow up with maximum sales conversions after the meeting?

I have a saying I live by and it's "Never meet a man on his own battlefield." - In other words, give yourself an unfair advantage - and it's by printing out this form and capturing someone's contact info on paper OR an electronic survey and pre-qualifying them while you educate someone on what it is you do and who you do it for.

Get My "Networking Without a Business Card Form & Survey Template

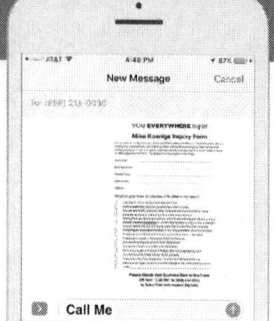

TEXT "CALLME" TO (858) 213-0030

You can see my survey right here: **www.YEN.tv/CallMe** - feel free to model it for your own business if you want.

The same basic information is on my "**Networking Without a Business Card Form**" located below.

Here's my live event sheet that I print out - go ahead and save this and modify it for your business: **www.YEN.tv/CallMeMike**.

Here's what I do when someone asks for my business card, I say:

> "I don't use business cards anymore. Let's face it, you'll give me yours, I'll give you mine and nothing is going to happen. Instead, take out your phone and text **CALLME** to (858) 213-0030."
>
> "Next, you're going to get a response and you can tell me more about you and what you need. You'll get my direct contact information and most importantly, I'LL FOLLOW UP AND HELP YOU!"

When they text their information, and see the results, they're impressed and they're ready to do business with me. That, and they'll probably want to know how this system works AND I have instant credibility and authority because I'm not like every other business coach, consultant or advisor.

And if you ARE a consultant, they might ask you to set them up with the same system! Boom! Instant paying client! You can adapt this strategy you're learning right now and get paid to set it up for someone else!

I'm going to repeat this using different language: if you DON'T have a business and are looking for something to offer a business person that's unique that you can charge $1,000-$5,000 for, you can set someone up with the scripts and follow up sequence I'm teaching you in this book. I've never met a business owner in my life who doesn't think their marketing and sales process needs help.

Keep reading - the next page has my "Networking Without a Business Card" form. You have my permission to model it for your business.

YOU EVERYWHERE NOW

Mike Koenigs Inquiry Form

Fill out this form to stay in touch, schedule a meeting with Mike or a Team Member to discuss building your audience with live streaming video, writing and publishing your best selling book, creating a product, show, infomercial, webcast/livecast, business coaching, studio rental or being on Mike's show at his $1mm+ You Everywhere Now studio in San Diego.

Your Name: _____

Business Name: _____

Mobile Phone: _____

Direct Email: _____

Website: _____

What do you want to discuss with Mike or his team?

- ☐ FOLLOW UP WITH ME During or After the Event!
- ☐ **Publish and Profit**: Become a Bestselling Author in 3 Days
- ☐ **Consult and Profit**: Generate Leads, Prospects and Close High-Ticket Deals
- ☐ **Speak and Profit**: Learn how to become a highly-paid speaker or learn how to speak and sell from stage and earn $10,000 - $100,000 or more per presentation

- ☐ **Create and Profit**: Learn how to rapidly produce information products and sell them with paid advertising and get a 2:1 daily ROI on advertising!
- ☐ **Celebrity Bootcamp**: Get a Sizzle Reel, Professional Interview, Get Promoted to Mike's Audience and Experience In-Studio Coaching and Mastermind Day
- ☐ **Product Creation Bootcamp**: In-Studio Step-By-Step Training on How to Set Up a Product Creation Studio and How to Make High-Quality Information Products
- ☐ **Produce an Information Product** at You Everywhere Now Studio in San Diego
- ☐ **Produce a Live Event** at the You Everywhere Now Studio in San Diego
- ☐ Produce a Livecast or Infomercial to Sell My Products
- ☐ Business Coaching with Mike to Grow My Business
- ☐ Have Mike Speak and/or Sell at My Next Event
- ☐ Rent the Studio to Produce a Product, Show or Livestreaming Event
- ☐ Hire Mike as Business Advisor for My Company
- ☐ Promote "You Everywhere Now" Products as an Affiliate/JV Partner
- ☐ Star as an Expert Guest on the Mike Koenigs or You Everywhere Now Show
- ☐ Other: _____

**Please Attach Your Business Card to this Form
OR Text "Call Me" to (858) 213-0030
to Enter This Information Digitally**

How to Get Better Clients, Close More Deals, Share Your Message, Build an Audience, Create a List, Multiply Your Income, Get Speaking Opportunities, Become Competition and Recession-Proof While Creating Expert, Celebrity, and Authority Status with the Most Powerful Marketing Tool in the World.

Get More Clients NOW

If YOU want to get attention, stand out and become a trusted person of influence, you NEED this masterclass RIGHT NOW to gain an unfair advantage and competitive edge to promote and market your business, reach celebrity status, attract better customers, make more money and help a lot of people.

Visit **www.YEN.tv/PAPWebinar** to watch the free training event right now.

More Example Video Proposals

These are real-world scripts you can model for your business. All of them are real and have closed deals ranging from $2,000 to $100,000. Each of these are real products that help business owners get found, get attention, get seen, heard, listened to, watched, read, anytime, anywhere, on demand, on any device.

For your reference, there are detailed descriptions of all of my offers at the end of this document so you can see how I adapt the message of a "pitch" for a specific market.

The majority of these product offers have sales web pages that you can examine, review and model for your own business. I encourage you to visit the web page they point to. This is an interactive exercise!

Example Script: Consult and Profit

Generate Leads, Prospects and Close High-Ticket Deals

Every business owner, entrepreneur or "wantrepreneur" I've ever met is always looking for an unfair advantage to influence, persuade, get and close more deals.

This example is designed to appeal to the largest number of entrepreneurs possible – from the total beginner who wants to reach $100k or more in sales in less than a year all the way to someone who already has a business that's earning millions of dollars more and knows they could do even better.

Let's assume at this point I've sent a couple "microcommitment" messages to you and you've indicated your interested in learning more about how to get and close deals faster, become more effective at influencing, persuading and generating leads.

This would be the follow up video I would send:

"Great. Here's the big idea. What would it be like to get paid $5,000-$30,000 a day for your time, experience, expertise, and story? Every business owner needs help. They all do. And the consulting and coaching market is a ½ Trillion dollar industry. I've helped hundreds of entrepreneurs break into the lucrative coaching and consulting market with little to no experience. All you need are the tools like forms, scripts, presentations, agreements, and the word-for-word training to get it all *done. We'll show you how to get qualified leads and close deals in as little as a day with nothing more than your mobile phone."*

Here's a link to watch a free masterclass that explains everything: http://www.yen.tv/CAPWebinar
OR
"I have five minutes right now if you want to jump on the phone and I'll explain the system to you and how you can use it to grow your business faster."

The next page is an explanation of the program – and some of the "hooks" we use that are used in our advertising, marketing and are adaptable to practically any business.

Free Masterclass - How to Get 3-5 High Ticket Consulting Deals Each Month With Reliability & Predictability... Even If You've NEVER Had A Consulting Client Before!

> **How To Get 3-5 High Ticket Consulting Deals Each Month With Reliability & Predictability...**
>
> Even If You've NEVER Had A Consulting Client Before!
> Join This Free Online Class ONLY If You Want To Get High Ticket Consulting Clients Faster & Easier Than You Ever Thought Possible...
>
> Yes! Sign Me Up & Send Me The Details >>

Here's SOME of What You'll Learn in this **Free Masterclass**:

1. A **single step-by-step lead generation and sales method that closed a $29,000, a $70,000, a $8,900 and an $18,500 deal** in two weeks that can be used in any business with no training, no experience, no software or special technology required.
2. You're going to discover how someone who failed Kindergarten (Ed Rush) became the #1 fighter pilot in the Marine Corps and how the same strategy he used can work for you to close bigger

deals for more money. NOTE - it's crazy...there is literally a 1-to-1 correlation of this "cockpit" strategy into business.

3. You'll find out the **6 main things that are holding you back from closing $10,000+ deals right now**. (Make sure to bring a pen and a pad of paper...these are important...and ONE will surprise you.)
4. A **step-by-step checklist - so that when you line these up, you are flat out guaranteed to start making money** and helping people.
5. NEW (never-before-seen-or-heard) Content. A **totally new approach to closing big consulting deals**. This approach called the "6-Figure Text Message" has been instrumental for us in **closing deals between $29,000 and $70,000**. You'll get the exact formula, word-for-word.
6. You'll see the result of 4 years of research that we call "**The 5 Most Lucrative Business Models.**" (One of these will surprise you.) These can create a major breakthrough for you when you implement them correctly even if you're in transition, reinventing yourself or don't have a business or product of your own.
7. The **"8 Words to Double Your Deals"** Technique. If you want to either: close more deals or close bigger deals, these 8 words are for you.

Visit **www.YEN.tv/CAPWebinar** right now - the next Masterclass is scheduled today.

Example Script:
Publish and Profit Live Event

Become a Bestselling Author in 3 Days

This example is a "no-brainer" for business owners and people who are struggling to get attention or get their foot in the door with prospects. The reason I'm sharing this example with you is because it's a complete strategy that shows you how to close a deal with one short video OR "push" the prospect into an automated marketing webinar that converts 15-25% of every lead into a buyer.

Here's the basic pitch and overview:

By FAR the most powerful way to establish expert and authority status, become an influencer, get speaking gigs, media attention, multiply your income while becoming competition and recession-proof is to write a book and become a bestselling author.

Many people mistakenly believe it takes months or years to write a book and become a bestselling author until they attend our 3-day "Publish and Profit" event or do our home-study course.

We're helped over 1,100 entrepreneurs become bestselling authors and it flat-out changes their lives and careers in days or weeks.

This is a "typical" conversation I have with a professional – and for the sake of consistency, I'm going to assume that the person I'm speaking to is a health professional.

"Hi _____ - great meeting you at the _____ event last week. You filled out my follow-up form and I looked at your web site today. It's clear to me that you want authority in the integrative medical market, you need some kind of tool to get leads for your new online course and get the 'right' kind of clients into your clinic. You also mentioned you want to get media appearances and speaking gigs. I know exactly what you need to make all of this happen and the great news is I can help you in only 3 days. What you need is a bestselling book. The great news is I have personally helped over 1,000 business owners, experts, consultants, advisors and coaches from 81 countries become best selling authors and I know I can help you too! It's a system called Publish and Profit and it's a one-stop resource for writing a book, creating great covers, coming up with compelling titles, and launching your book in paperback and Kindle formats. If you've never written a book, this is the fastest way to get that published. If you already have a book, but it didn't help you grow your business, we can help you re-launch your book and become a best selling author. I've included a link to a 5 minute video, examples of bestsellers in the medical field and some testimonials from past customers in your field. We only have 9 seats left and every events sells out!"
Here's that link: www.YEN.tv/Publish

The next segment describes the product in detail.

The Most Powerful Tool in the World to Get Better Clients, Close More Deals, Share Your Message, Build an Audience, Multiply Your Income, Get Speaking Opportunities, Gain Celebrity & Authority Status and Become Competition and Recession-Proof

If you want to stand out, you need the **single most powerful tool to gain a competitive edge, promote and market your business, reach celebrity status, attract better customers, make more money** and help a lot of people too.

Best of all, there are hundreds of years of **irrefutable proof that this works in any business or industry, online and offline, in any language, anywhere in the world**.

What is this magical tool? It's a book. Your book. But It's not about the book; it's about the power it will give you.

With a published book, you can **access almost the entire human race**, connect with your perfect audience, share your message, sell more products, create buzz, and have real authority and credibility in any market.

It's one of the few ways to get your prospects to take you to bed with them! ;)

Have you dreamed of writing and publishing a book that's the sum total of your expertise to attract paying clients...but you never even got started because it always seems too hard? Maybe you tell yourself, "it will take me years to do...how do I organize it, or even start to design a book cover?" You tell yourself you'll never be able to get it done, so why even try?

The system is called Publish and Profit that will lead you step-by-step through a system that has helped over 1,000 business owners write, publish, and profit from books in as little as TWO weeks. Our youngest author, Abby Richter, wrote four books in only 3 months when she was just 9 years old! We have customers in their 80's too. You don't need to be a writer to be a successful author.

To learn more, visit **www.YEN.tv/PAPWebinar** and if you have any questions, call (858) 227-9108 x102 or email **Support@YouEverywhereNow.com**

Example Script: Celebrity Bootcamp

Learn How to Be Comfortable on Camera, Get Media Trained, Create a Professional Media Package, Get a Sizzle Reel, a Professional Interview and Get Promoted to Mike's Audience, LIVE from the Million-Dollar You Everywhere Now Studio in San Diego in Only 3 Days!

For us, the natural "progression" in our sales funnel is to help our customers become better influencers and close more deals in the coaching, consulting or advising space (Consult and Profit).

Next, we help them establish authority, credibility, expert and celebrity status with Publish and Profit.

Next, we supercharge their celebrity status by giving them what appears to be 18-36 months worth of on-camera experience, photographs, interviews, a "sizzle reel" and everything else they might want so they can get on TV, traditional media, get interviews, paid speaking gigs and more. We call this the "Celebrity Bootcamp".

Visit **www.YEN.tv/Bootcamp** to see this product offer and watch a brief sales video. Pay attention to how the script and offer are described so you can model it for your business.

Step 1: Context, Framing and "I heard you and know what's wrong"

"Hi ____ - you and I met at JJ Virgin's event. You told me that you're struggling to get good leads, close deals with high-quality customers, attract the attention of live event promoters to get speaking gigs, get media attention and tell your story or elevator pitch effectively. You also mentioned you're scared to make your own videos and are confused about how to start using Facebook Live to promote yourself and your business. I have an idea I'm certain will help you solve these challenges. It's a quick way to generate qualified leads, get Facebook traffic and promote your book and coaching business. If you want to know more, just text me back and I'll send you a 1 minute video that will show you everything you need to know."

Step 2: The Pitch (this can be pre-recorded)

"I'm glad you asked for this video. Here's the big idea - and it's going to help you get attention, get on stages, close more deals and finally start generating leads on Facebook in less than 3 days. It's a way for you to get media trained so you're camera confident, get a sizzle reel to close speaking deals and get on stages, get a great video to use on social media, look like you've been on TV for 3 years, get professional photos, a video infomercial that establishes your credibility, authority and celebrity status AND a lead generation tool that you can use to promote your book, products, services and business. When someone from the media sees this, they'll want to put you on their show because you have instant authority and credibility. It's a program called 'The Celebrity Bootcamp'. I'll get you camera confident in one day and

promote you to my social following so you get leads and sales immediately. I've shared a link so you can see some example videos, sizzle reels and interviews, testimonials and from some past customers who were exactly where you are now. We have an event scheduled next month but you'll want to hurry because there are only 3 seats available. Click the link and text me back if you have any questions."

Here's the link: www.YEN.tv/Bootcamp

On the next page, you can read a detailed description of this offer so you can get a feel for how the pitch script is written.

Don't worry if it takes you a while to "get your head around" some of the scripting — it takes time to get fully immersed in this but you'll catch on quickly.

It took me years to figure out how to compress an hour worth of sales material inside 1-2 minutes!

The next block of text is the product description and "reason why" someone would want to join.

Become a Celebrity in Only 48 Hours!

Let's face it. We live in a **celebrity-driven "popularity contest"** world where it's almost impossible to get the attention of your ideal prospect or customer.

How are **you going to stand out, get noticed, get attention, create buzz and even get a CHANCE to share your message, engage a group** or an individual long enough to START building a relationship?

HOW?

You've got to take matters into your own hands. You need to do what every celebrity in the world has done - including the **Kardashians, Donald Trump, Oprah** and virtually other superstar celebrity has done...

WHAT'S THAT YOU ASK?

Manufacture Your Own Celebrity!

You've heard the old saying, **"fake it 'til you make it"**, right?

Here's what you need in to stand out and live the **"You Everywhere Now" dream** of getting attention, found, seen, heard, watched, read, on any device, anywhere, anytime and on demand.

If you want to stand out, get attention, attract better customers, close more deals and increase your profits without doing more work in this noisy, overwhelmed planet while everyone is staring at their phones all day with an attention span that's shorter than a goldfish...then you need a "Celebrity Toolkit" that forces an audience to pay attention to you and packages you like a pro.

Here's what you need in your "Celebrity Toolkit" to stand out and get attention:

- A **media kit** including celebrity-quality **photos and headshots**
- A **"sizzle reel" that makes you look like you're a pro on camera**, comfortable giving interviews, like you've been on TV for years. *If you're not comfortable on camera, speaking publicly or have never been on stage, you'll look and sound like a pro in no time! Mike has coached over 100,000 people online and thousands in person on overcoming their fears!*
- A polished **30-second "elevator speech"** that grabs attention and tells your prospect who you are, what you do, who you do it for and why they should pay attention and listen to you

- A **short, 4-8 minute, high-quality television-quality, interview-style mini-infomercial** video where you can share your story, share your business and provide a "call to action" to get people to get in touch with you NOW, not tomorrow, next week or next month
- You'll learn everything you need to know to **"Go Live" with Facebook Live** from your own home or office studio, even if you aren't a techie
- And you need to get **PROMOTED online**!

Watch this video at **www.YEN.tv/Bootcamp** to see real-life examples and a breakdown of what all of this looks like and how it's possible to "manufacture celebrity" in as little as 48 hours - even though it typically takes most people 18-36 months (or longer) to do!

And if you want to take action and shorten the cycle yourself, check out the **Celebrity Bootcamp** at **www.yen.tv/Bootcamp** where you can go behind the scenes, get professional coaching, masterminding and walk away with a complete celebrity package and get promoted to Mike's entire social following!

If you have any questions, call (858) 227-9108 x102 or email **Support@YouEverywhereNow.com**

Example Script: Speak and Profit

Learning how to become a paid or platform speaker is the most valuable skill you can learn and Speak and Profit is the system to help you gain those skills in days instead of years.

I need to give you a bit of a backstory before giving you the scripts I use to sell Speak and Profit. I think this is important because most people have a "story" as to why they can't or don't want to speak. We've all heard that quote about how speaking in public is in the top 3 things people are most afraid of. Almost everyone has a traumatic story – and here's mine:

When I was 5 years old, a bunch of kids made fun of me for singing with my dad in kindergarten at "show and tell" day. He's an excellent guitarist, performer and entertainer. He's always been my hero. That experience traumatized me and for about 20 years, I never spoke in public and stayed "behind the camera" instead. It's one of the reasons I became a programmer.

In my 30's, I would speak in front of businesspeople and very small groups, but in 2003, everything changed.

I produced my first information product, "The Internet Infomercial Toolkit." Because of that product, I was suddenly one of the world's experts on the subject of selling with online video.

One of my customers contacted me and asked if I would speak to a room of entrepreneurs about how to use online video to get and close deals.

I wasn't paid to speak, rather, I could present, sell my product, keep half the money and the other half went to the event producer. He told me I needed an order form – so he gave me one to model, I added the features and benefits of the program and a special price: $997.

There were 81 people in that room. 24 of them bought the Infomercial Toolkit for $997. Total sales: $23,928. 50% of that was $11,964. That was mine – minus travel and expenses.

Not bad for 75 minutes of "work"! I was hooked. Since then, I've spoken hundreds of times, in Malaysia, England, Australia, Canada, Mexico and have been asked to speak in China, Ireland, South Africa and France.

On several occasions, I've spoken on stages with over 1,000 people in the audience and "converted" more than half of the attendees into customers with offers of $3,000 or more, grossing over $500,000 in less than two hours.

Once I started speaking publicly, my business grew dramatically. The more I spoke, the more speaking opportunities came my way. I decided it was time to produce my own event…

My team and I put together a plan and offer, emailed it to all of my customers and asked everyone I know to invite their customers to our event, "The Firepower Business Builder Blueprint."

At that event, we got 242 customers in the room. Each paid $297 to attend. And over a period of three days, we sold some of our own programs for $1,997. 46% of the people bought our product resulting in sales of:

242 * $297 = $71,874
242 * 46% close rate = 111 sales * $1997 = $221,667
Total event sales: $293,541

Over the course of nearly 15 years, I've produced over 50 events. To the best of my knowledge, I was the first (or one of the first) people to ever sell a $100,000 product from stage in the "online marketing" niche.

Fast forward to 2012, I was diagnosed with cancer and brought in my good friend, Ed Rush, to take my place while I was treated for the next 9 months. He's a really effective speaker, presenter and salesperson on stage AND he does "paid speaking" – getting $7,500-$15,000 per appearance plus expenses.

There's much more to this story, but the bottom line is over the past 5 years, Ed and I have produced over 20 products and events together and sold over $12,000,000 (twelve million dollars) in revenue.

Even though we "accidently" helped a lot of people become successful speakers and presenters with our training programs, we wanted to make a dedicated product that specifically taught speaking skills. Together, we decided to turn our experience and knowledge into a product, "Speak and Profit" to help entrepreneurs, authors, consultants, coaches and small business owners into paid or platform speakers quickly.

So why should you care about this story and how will Speak and Profit help you?

In less than two days, Ed and I will teach you everything you need to know about how to craft a "signature talk", how to build and grow a paid or platform speaking skillset so that you can get and close deals quickly.

Speaking is, pound for pound, hour for hour, dollar for dollar, the single most effective way to earn more money, gain leverage, attention, influence, build, engage and grow an audience and improve your lifestyle.

Without exception, everyone I've ever met who has learned how to speak and get paid earn more, impact more people and achieve a higher standard and quality of life.

What follows are the scripts I use to get the interest of a prospect and convert them into a Speak and Profit customer.

Step 1: Context, Framing and "I heard you and know what's wrong"

"Hi _____ - you and I met at Joe Polish's Genius Network event after I spoke. You mentioned you wanted to speak on stages and asked me for some tips about how to get on stage, how to get the attention of a promoter, what to sell and how much you should sell your products for. You also asked for my advice as to whether you should do paid speaking or learn how to sell from the platform first. I did some research on you, checked out your web site and have a few ideas for you on how you can start speaking quickly. You have a book, a health coaching business and you have a treatment center. The good news is speaking will definitely help you grow your business. I I have all of the tools, scripts, templates and contracts you need to book gigs quickly. Speaking is the most effective way to promote your book, sell your services and grow your consulting / coaching / advising business. If you want to know more about my system, just text me back and I'll send you a 1 minute video with my ideas and recommendations."

Step 2: The Pitch

*"Awesome! Based on our conversation, you want to put together an awesome presentation, get booked, get paid speaking fees, sell your books, consulting services, and host your own events. You need a system that will help you make a "signature" talk that can be as short as 10 minutes or longer than an hour that will educate, entertain and engage an audience and get the attention of event producers and promoters. You'll get the exact word-for-word scripts to help you pitch, influence, persuade and

close deals from $10 books to $100,000 offers. You'll get speaking templates, pitch letters, emails, proposals, agreements, contracts, scripts and strategies. You'll get the exact system and process you need to earn hundreds of thousands or millions of dollars per year. I'll even review your speech and promote you to my audience! The system is called Speak and Profit. You'll get every tool and system that I've used to sell millions of dollars of products and get on stages including Tony Robbins, "The Wolf of Wall Street" Jordan Belfort, JJ Virgin, Brian Tracy, John Assaraf and dozens more.

Below this video is a link so you can watch a short video and some testimonials from some past customers who were exactly where you are now. You're obviously an action-taker, so here's everything you need to know to start, build and grow your speaking business QUICKLY. Because you reached out to me personally, I'm willing to give you a 15% discount when you register right now. The discount is only for today."

Here's the link: http://www.YEN.tv/Speak

That's the pitch. Like all the other scripts, I modify it to suit the prospect and reflect their challenges so they know I understand who they are, what they need and make sure the follow up video is self-contained so it can be shared with a decision-maker. I include a reason to make a decision NOW.

Learn the Most Valuable Skill that Produces Bigger, Faster Deals & Income Per Hour than Anything

Being a paid or platform speaker is the most valuable skill you can learn and Speak and Profit is the system to help you learn those skills in record time.

Speak and Profit is a step-by-step system, based on the combined experience of millionaire speakers, Mike Koenigs and Ed Rush. Mike has been speaking and selling from the platform for over 15 years. Ed has been speaking for 10 years both as a "platform" and fee-based speaker.

Speak and Profit includes step-by-step tools to help you create and prepare your pitch and presentation, how to create an offer that converts like crazy, how to promote yourself, how to perform and profit as a speaker.

The program includes speaking templates, inquiry emails to get booked as a paid speaker, scripts, how to convert from stage, how to raise money for nonprofits and charities, how to build a list from stage and much more. Ed and Mike guide you through product offers from $500-$100,000, how to sell books, products, services and masterminds.

Learn more at **www.YEN.tv/Speak**, send a message to **Sales@YouEverywhereNow.com** OR call (858) 227-9108 x102.

Example Script: Create and Profit

Step-By-Step Training on How to Set Up a Product Creation Studio and How to Make High-Quality Information Products.

The majority of our clients want to learn how to turn their knowledge, wisdom, experience and expertise into a product, create automated sales funnels, start advertising on Facebook and make money while they sleep. I certainly do!

The good news is I've been marketing online since 1994, before there was an Internet to speak of and have taught over 50,000 people in 121 countries how to do it for themselves.

Create and Profit represents over 20 years of compressed knowledge in an easy to digest course that guides someone with expert knowledge how to do it step-by-step. The system is adaptable to any business type.

In this example, I'm going to pitch an integrative doctor I met at a live event. I've worked with thousands of doctors, nutritionists, people from the healing arts, psychiatrists, psychologists and everything in between. Without exception, they feel beaten down by the system, are overworked, underpaid and LOVE helping and healing people but are positively sick of dealing with bureaucracy, insurance and overregulation and legislation by state and federal governments.

In a perfect world, they'd like to find a way to keep their high-end clientele, continue to serve but run a cash business, quit taking insurance and turn their knowledge, wisdom, experience and expertise into information products and coach patients instead of doing in-patient treatments.

Many doctors would also like to train other doctors and provide certification programs, paid speaking and travel.

Step 1: Context, Framing and "I heard you and know what's wrong"

"Hi _____ - great meeting you at JJ Virgin's event last week. You and I talked about how you are frustrated with your practice and are sick of dealing with the bureaucracy and hassles of insurance. I've been thinking about you and have an idea that will help you reinvent yourself and grow your business. You mentioned to me that you have been training other integrated doctors how to run a profitable holistic clinic as a business and you have three really great case studies of docs you've trained who have tripled their revenue in just 18 months. I have an idea that will help you turn your experience into a scalable business so you can get away from your normal practice - and put $30k-$80k or more in your pocket without doing a lot of extra work. Just text me back and I'll send you a short 1 minute video of what I'm thinking about for you."

BTW - this is a REAL LIFE example of an everyday occurrence for me! So many business owners have been doing the same things for decades, have sustainable businesses and are mentoring or advising other people on how to do what they've done successfully but haven't turned their advice or consulting into a big-ticket product. This is a perfect solution for them!

This short video will get his attention and get him super interested (and committed) in moving forward. In fact, I'll just reply with the video and a link to register for the course!

Step 2: The Pitch (this can be pre-recorded)

"I'm glad you responded. Here's the idea I have for you - and the result is you'll be able to turn what you're already doing into a certification program that you can sell to other doctors and practitioners for $5k-$10k or even more, make money from day one and quickly get away from the day-to-day hassle of running your clinic and dealing with insurance hassles and state regulations and bureaucracy. This system will show you everything you need to know to create a recurring income stream that you can quickly scale. It's something we call Create and Profit. You'll see step-by-step how to create an information product. I'll show you how to set up a home or office studio for less than $2,000 and demonstrate step-by-step how to create your product, make a membership site and promote it with Facebook Live and Facebook Ads. We'll show you how you can get paid to make the product - and create all the social proof you need from past customers so your program will practically sell itself. And then we'll show you how you can incorporate coaching and masterminds to build a recurring income stream. Best of all, you can have as many of your staff members watch how this is done so they can help you. You'll walk away

and know exactly how everything works without having to become a tech-nerd. Here's the link to register – and don't hesitate to reply with any questions you might have. Hurry though, the price of the program increases $1,000 this Sunday!"

Here's the link: http://www.yen.tv/Create

Now - there's a LOT to this script, but the bottom line is I help the viewer VISUALIZE themselves being there and I overcame just about every possible objection including the "I'm not technical" or "can a team member watch it with me?", "how am I going to make money?", "I don't have a studio."

Notice I included a deadline – the price increases $1,000 on Sunday and a specific call to action.

Once you start speaking to a few prospects, they tell you everything they want and need and what they're afraid of or hesitant about. I make a point of overcoming every possible objection in my short video replies.

What follows is a description of Create and Profit.

How to Make Profitable Products in Only 48 Hours

It's REALLY easy to turn your ideas into high-priced products or books that pay you over and over again when you use a repeatable systematic formula.

In this video, Mike will guide you through the 10x10 Content Creation Formula that he's used repeatedly to turn his **ideas into books and 6 and 7-figure products in 100 days or less**.

Watch this video at **http://www.yen.tv/Create** for an easy exercise you can use to pull your personal wisdom, expertise, knowledge and know-how into a #1

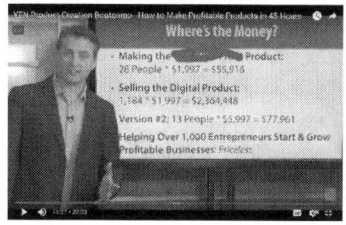

bestselling book, high-priced product, consulting, coaching or advisor program that you can sell with Facebook ads and automated webinars. Mike will also guide you through **three case studies of products that were produced and have been responsible for earning multiple 7-figures in less than 100 days**.

How would you like to learn how to **make, market and launch information products**, build marketing funnels and **promote your products and services with Facebook Ads and Facebook Live in just two days** so you can turn your knowledge, wisdom and expertise into high-priced information products and **get paid BEFORE they're even made**?

Watch this video about Create and Profit at **http://www.yen.tv/Create**. For more information or to talk to someone on our team, send an email message to **Sales@YouEverywhereNow.com** OR call (858) 227-9108 x102. Remember - Money Loves Speed and Time Kills Deals!

Summary, Implementation and Action Steps

"Money Loves Speed and Time Kills Deals."

My goal for you in this chapter is to motivate and inspire you to take action and make an extra $1,000 - $5,000 or $10,000 in the next few days. It's possible when you **take action and IMPLEMENT**.

I know this to be true because after building and selling two businesses to publicly-traded companies and four more for cash, earning nearly $50,000,000 online, serving nearly 50,000 customers in over 100 countries, I wish I knew 20 years ago what I've shared with you in this short book.

I know it's not easy to get motivated, start, build and grow a business profitably while maintaining your health, sanity, marriage, relationship with your kids, staying balanced, happy and having a sound spiritual life.

But it's entirely possible to take a few shortcuts that can and will get you RESULTS and earn more money faster without spending all the time and effort it normally takes to create products, build services, build a list, do advertising, hire and train employees and deal with an overreaching government.

HOW? Just go out and hustle. The sooner you start talking to people and building momentum, the sooner you'll make money and it's just not that hard. My last two companies took me 10 years each to build and sell. My latest company only took a year to build from scratch to over $2,000,000 in sales and the next year has a delta that will exceed $6,000,000 and likely $12,000,000 over more in the 3rd year. No investors, no banks, no loans.

If all you did was find a company that would pay you 10%-20% to bring paying customers to them using the strategies outlined in this book you could make tens or hundreds of thousands of dollars a month, starting in less than a week. I'm talking no overhead, no employees, no fulfillment, no delivery. Or if you do have a company, this is the pathway to profitability. Fast.

I'm not telling you this to impress you, but to impress upon you how important getting and staying motivated is - and it begins with getting in a mindset of hustle and closing deals.

In closing - I encourage you to drop me a message at **MikeKoenigs@gmail.com**, visit my web site at **www.YouEverywhereNow.com** and attend one of my free training webinars to help you build and grow your audience, following, get attention and make a big difference in the world.

As I said in the beginning of this chapter, "Money Loves Speed and Time Kills Deals."

Get out there and implement and keep me posted on your progress!

Mike

PS - If you want to **Get 3-5 High Ticket Consulting Deals Each Month with Reliability & Predictability**...Even If You've NEVER Had A Consulting Client Before, **register here at www.yen.tv/CAPWebinar**

PPS - make sure you visit me on **Facebook and post a comment or video about how much you like Money Phone, ok?**

PPPS - I want to help get You Everywhere Now! GoLive and Profit will help you get attention, found, seen, heard, watched & read on any device, anytime, anywhere & on demand! **www.YEN.tv/GoLive**!

Make $$$ with Webcasts, Webinars & Facebook Live!

Get Webcast Profit Toolkit right now for 81% off!

I rarely (if ever) do this, but right now, you can get Webcast Profit Toolkit system for 81% off right now. Can you say "Bonus!?!?

This program has sold for as much as $2,497.00 - so you're getting everything at a tiny fraction of that price (you can get started for less than $500).

Check out this page where I explain everything.

Why are we doing this very limited sale?

Because today marks the anniversary of my wildly popular Webcast Profit Toolkit system - the same program that has helped hundreds of business owners (just like you) discover how to create instant credibility and fame with online video.

Listen...I could walk from San Diego to Maine on top of success stories from this program.

So...I am going to bend over backwards to get it into your hands...to the tune of 81% off.

Webcast Profit Toolkit includes an incredible program that includes live case studies, and everything you need to start "broadcasting" your message to the world. Think about it - in just a few days, you could have your own LIVE or recorded show.

Think you need a lot of gear? **Think again.**
I'll show you how to get up, running, and profitable with nothing more than your laptop.

But you *must act now* - I'm only leaving this offer up for a super short period of time.

The HALF OFF sale ends midnight this Saturday at midnight. And **when you <u>enroll right now</u>**, you'll get INSTANT ACCESS to the entire system.

<u>**Go here to find out more**</u> - discounted 81%!

Plus, when you enroll in Webcast Profit Toolkit before midnight on Saturday, you get 21 additional "FAST ACTION" bonuses including...

- **Bonus #1: "Million Dollar Day" Tools and Templates:** Everything you need to Prepare, Produce, Perform, Promote & Profit from webcasts including lead capture pages, email promotion copy, event pages & show flow. These "swipe files" alone took years to create, cost over $250,000, and produced millions of dollars in income! This is a massively valuable bonus!

- **Bonus #2: Webcast Profit Toolkit Masterclass:** You'll get access to a Virtual Interactive Training Bootcamp where you'll learn step-by-step how to do live interactive programs, create a product from scratch, set up cameras, equipment and answer questions.

- **Bonus #3 - $10,000 in Less than 12 minutes:** The secret "countdown" video formula that sells for you. Three scripts valued over $10,000 each that have produced over $1,000,000 in sales you can model for your own programs.

PLUS, there are 18 more (count 'em!) bonuses **on this page** at **www.YEN.tv/WPTK**.

All told, with your special discount, you're saving 81% off the standard Webcast Profit Toolkit rate!

That's like making the smartest possible investment in your future…for a tiny fraction of the price. :)

Here's your link - **www.YEN.tv/WPTK** to get going with Webcast Profit Toolkit, and in just minutes, you'll be inside with the entire system!

Talk soon,
Mike

Where's the Money This Year? Join us for a Business, Marketing, Opportunities & Tech Predictions Show to Grow Your Business!

MIKE DROP! The 5th Annual Business, Marketing, Opportunities, Tech, Gadgets Predictions Presentation is READY for you NOW at **www.YEN.tv/Predictions** **(during the presentation, you'll get a 121 page manual with all the slides, notes, links and resources FREE! :)**

Here's what you'll experience at this free event:

- **The Future**: Where are the Opportunities & Money this year?
- **CASE STUDY #1**: The Email + 10 Minute Video that Made $97,970 in 7 Days (you get the emails, scripts and video to model for your own business)
- **"Best of CES" Tour** + Tech/Gadget Trends Report
- **DEMO**: Video Equipment Recommendations for Facebook Live & Video Marketing

- **Ed Rush**: How to Close More Deals, Attract Better Customers (and Repel The Wrong Ones) with Radical Transparency
- **CASE STUDY #2**: How We are Getting a 2:1-4:1 on Our Advertising Investment in ONE DAY (I'll give you the ads, the emails, lead capture pages and access to the marketing funnel that earns every day!)
- **How to "Hack Celebrity"**, Build an Audience, Grow a List and Triple Your Prices in 3 Days
- **Five Must-Read Book** Recommendations to Grow Your Business
- **TWO Marketing Hacks** that have increased our sales 15% in our business overall that you can completely swipe! One for Facebook, the other works in any business!

And - we give away portable studios (and show you what the best gear is for portable recording with a smartphone including selfie sticks, lights, microphones, tripods and a great lighting rig that will *make you look like a celebrity*!)

Plus on the webcast, you'll get **ALL the Notes & Slides, free**!

Get access to the masterclass right now by visiting **www.YEN.tv/Predictions**

It's Time for You to Go Live and Profit!

If you want to stand out, get attention, attract better customers, close more deals and increase your profits without doing more work, then this is what you need RIGHT NOW to **build an audience, list, engage and convert them into paying customers with Facebook Live, mobile marketing and automation**.

Perhaps you noticed I'm wearing a gold outfit.
DID I GET YOUR ATTENTION?

A study by **Microsoft published in Time magazine** reported that in the year 2000 **the average human attention span had dropped from 12 seconds to eight seconds**.

A goldfish has a **nine second attention span**.

In the world of marketing, **you have 2 seconds to grab someone's attention**.

If they're interested in what they see or hear, you might get **20 seconds of their time**.
If that's good, you'll get **2 minutes**.

And if you earn 20 minutes of someone's time, you can probably **influence and persuade almost anyone to begin a relationship and buy something from you**.

Here's an important question:
How are you going to stand out, get attention and close deals on this noisy, overwhelmed planet while everyone is staring at their phones all day with an attention span that's shorter than a goldfish?

Listen, money loves speed and time kills deals.

So I'm not going to waste yours or my time.

©2017 Mike Koenigs and You Everywhere Now
Get the Free Money Phone Bonus Video at www.GoMoneyPhone.com

But if you give me 2 minutes, I'll show and tell you exactly what you need to get someone's attention and time.

The entire planet is obsessed with their smartphones and billions are sold every year.
In case you haven't noticed, nearly everyone is experiencing an augmented reality, staring at and thumbing through texts, emails, Facebook, Instagram, Snapchat and WhatsApp.

Facebook has nearly **2 billion users** and **over 1 billion of them** login and create **4.5 BILLION pieces of information** and lives EVERY DAY!

The recent explosion of Facebook Live put a mobile television studio into billions of people's pockets. If you understand a few secrets, you can completely change the way you do business. **But if you don't, you or your business can become irrelevant, especially to the next generation of consumers**.

Successful business owners, entrepreneurs and entertainers all have one BIG thing in common:

They know how to **disrupt the status quo, get attention, present the right message to the right market**, at the right time and in the right place.

What if you could get EXACTLY what you need in one place - every tool, resource, all the knowledge you need to future-prepare, future proof, and guide you step-by-step through how to start, build or grow a business that leverages the latest "what's working now and proven to get results systems" without spending weeks, months or years and thousands of dollars?

Introducing GoLive and Profit.

Learn more - watch this short video that describes the system at **www.YEN.tv/GoLive**

About Mike Koenigs

Originally from tiny Eagle Lake, Minnesota (population 763), Mike barely passed high school, never went to college but taught himself how to program and write video games when he was 14 to escape his small-town roots and become a serial entrepreneur, building software and training programs to help entrepreneurs get attention, found, seen, heard, watched and read on any device, anytime, anywhere and on demand.

For Mike, it's not all about the money - he's raised over $2.4mm for his wife Vivian's "Just Like My Child" foundation. He's also a stage 3a cancer survivor, completing 9 months of chemotherapy and 33 radiation treatments. His doctors say he's healthy and cancer-free.

He's an eleven-time #1 Bestselling Author, "Marketer of the Year" winner, serial entrepreneur, filmmaker, international speaker, and patented inventor. His products have simplified and automated marketing for over 47,000 small businesses, authors, experts, speakers, coaches and consultants in over 100 countries.

Mike has built and sold his last two businesses to publicly-traded companies, including his most recent exits, Traffic Geyser and Instant Customer. His first company, Digital Cafe was sold to the publicly-traded Interpublic Group.

Since 2008, Mike Koenigs is known for producing 12 consecutive multi-million dollar product launches, earning over $44 million dollars in sales. His largest launch grossed over $9.1 million dollars in one week. Mike produced over $3.1 million dollars in a single "direct to camera" interactive online livecast.

He lives on the beach in La Jolla San Diego with his wife and son, Zak.

He can be reached at his personal web site at www.MrBz.com or business site at www.YouEverywhereNow.com.

Twitter: @MikeKoenigs
Facebook: www.Facebook.com/Koenigs (Fan Page)
 www.Facebook.com/MikeAKoenigs (Personal Page)
Meet Mike - Watch His Sizzle Reel Here:
www.YEN.tv/Sizzle

Book Mike Koenigs to Speak

Book Mike Koenigs as your Keynote Speaker and You're Guaranteed to Make Your Event Inspirational, Motivational, Highly Entertaining and Unforgettable!

For over two decades, Mike Koenigs has been educating, entertaining, motivating and inspiring business owners, entrepreneurs, authors, experts, speakers, consultants and coaches build and grow their businesses with the online video, social media, mobile and product creation strategies.

His origin story includes his recent near-death brush with stage 3a cancer, growing up lower middle-class in a small town in Eagle Lake Minnesota, severe ADHD and "meeting" Tony Robbins through an infomercial that changed his life forever. After successfully building and exiting from two companies and selling them to publicly-traded companies, Mike can share relevant, actionable strategies that anyone can use - even if they're starting from scratch.

His unique style inspires, empowers and entertains audiences while giving them the tools and strategies they need and want to get seen, heard, build and grow successful sustainable brands and businesses.

For more info and to book Mike for your next event, visit **www.MrBz.com/Speaking OR**, call or text +1 (858) 412-0858.

Will You Leave a Book Review?

Did you enjoy this book and find it useful? I will be very grateful when you posted a short review and your success story on Amazon right now!

Your support makes a difference and I *read and respond to all the reviews personally* to make this book even better!

To leave a review right now, go here: www.YEN.tv/MoneyPhoneReview

---

⭐⭐⭐⭐⭐ A Great Book Showing How To Turn Your Smartphone Into A Marketing Machine, By A Master Marketer

By Claude Whitacre author on February 1, 2017

Format: Paperback   Verified Purchase

Ok, I'm not a friend of the author, and am not a student of his. This is a real review of the book. I bought the hard copy.

To get the most out of this book, you need to look at it from two points of view. First, the content of the book, what you learn. Keonigs essentially tells you that "working an event" is a great way to prospect. I can promise you, this is true. Meeting people at events (on marketing, or for businesspeople) is a very select group of people that are used to spending money at events. You almost can't get a better prospect, if you are selling to the niche that attends. The more they paid to attend the event, the better. But you can still get great results at free events.

I know three marketers that go to large marketing events about three or four times a year. And that's the only prospecting they need to do. It's that effective.

Then the author gives you every single template you need to meet the prospects, what to say....everything, and then use your phone to send them texts and videos, culminating in a high ends sale a few days later. I know these techniques work. I've used them in the past to make
sales, and they have been used to make sales to me. The methods are sound.

∨ Read more

2 comments   23 people found this helpful. Was this review helpful to you?   Report abuse

Made in the USA
San Bernardino, CA
11 April 2019